AF584795

Australian States *and Territories*

WESTERN AUSTRALIA

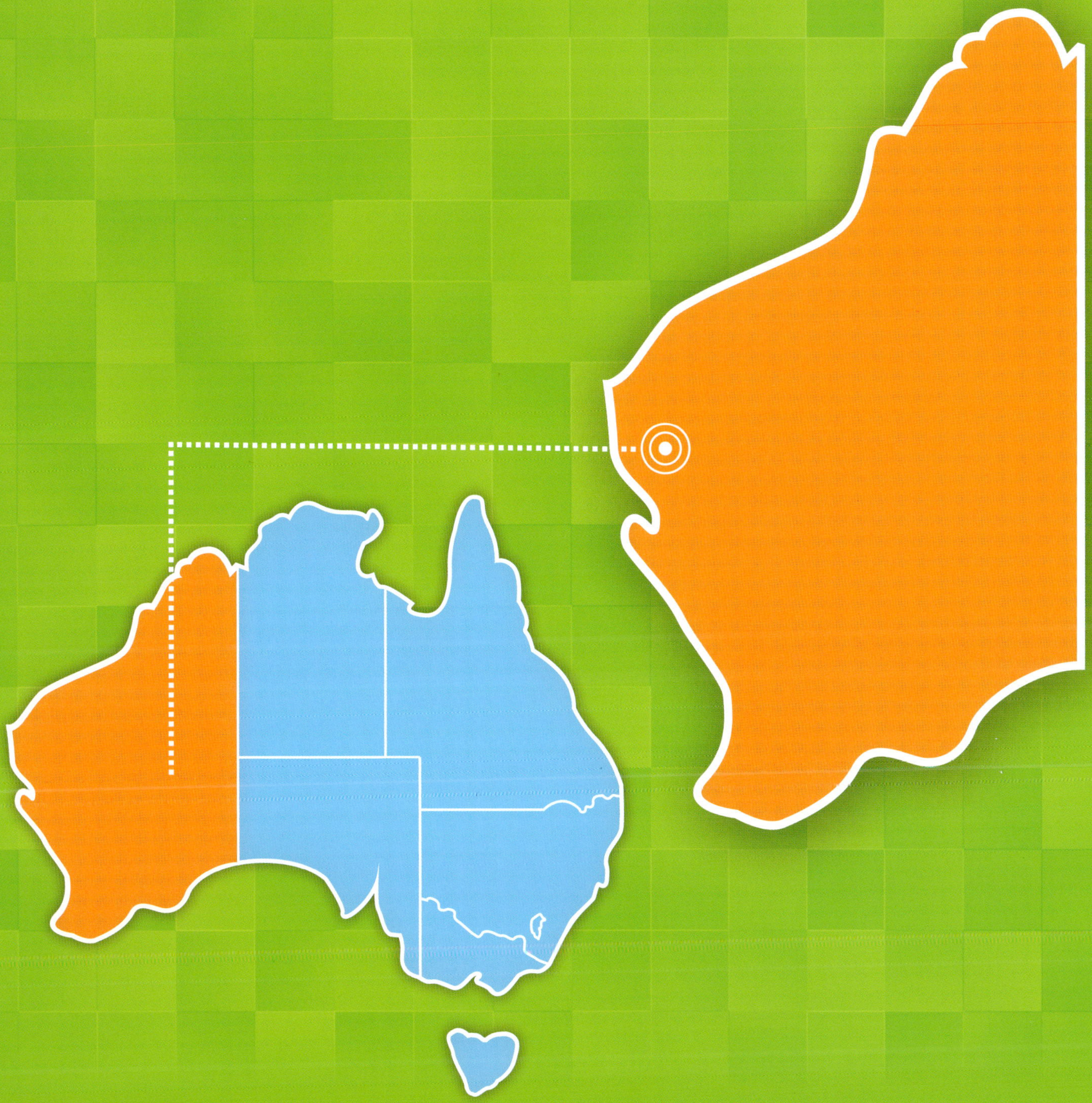

Linsie Tan

Redback Publishing
PO Box 357 Frenchs Forest NSW 2086
Australia

ISBN 978-0-9946247-7-2

First published 2017
Reprinted 2018

Author: Linsie Tan
Editor: Jane Hinchey
Original illustrations © Redback Publishing 2017
Originated by Redback Publishing
Printed and bound in China by Leo Paper

Acknowledgements
We would like to thank the following for permission to reproduce photographs: State Library of Western Australia, George Pitt Morison, National Library of Australia PIC Drawer 1651 #S1139, PIC/8381/337 LOC Album 1054/D, PIC Album 1235 #PIC/18177/13, PIC/12321/3 LOC Cold Store PIC POS, State Library of NSW, kikujungboy / Shutterstock.com, Dylan Lodge, Cgoodwin, Jessica Lawrence, Eurofins Agroscience Services, Nachoman-au, Australian Paralympic Committee, Stefan Tell, Mitchell Library, State Library of New South Wales, State Heritage Office, Andrea Izzotti / Shutterstock.com, ingehogenbijl / Shutterstock.com, CSIRO, By Johannes van Keulen, Georgios Kollidas / Shutterstock.com, Michaela De Freitas / Shutterstock.com.

Every effort has been made to contact copyright holders of any material reproduced in this book. Any omissions will be rectified in subsequent printings if notice is given to the publisher.

Cataloguing-in-Publication details are available from the National Library of Australia

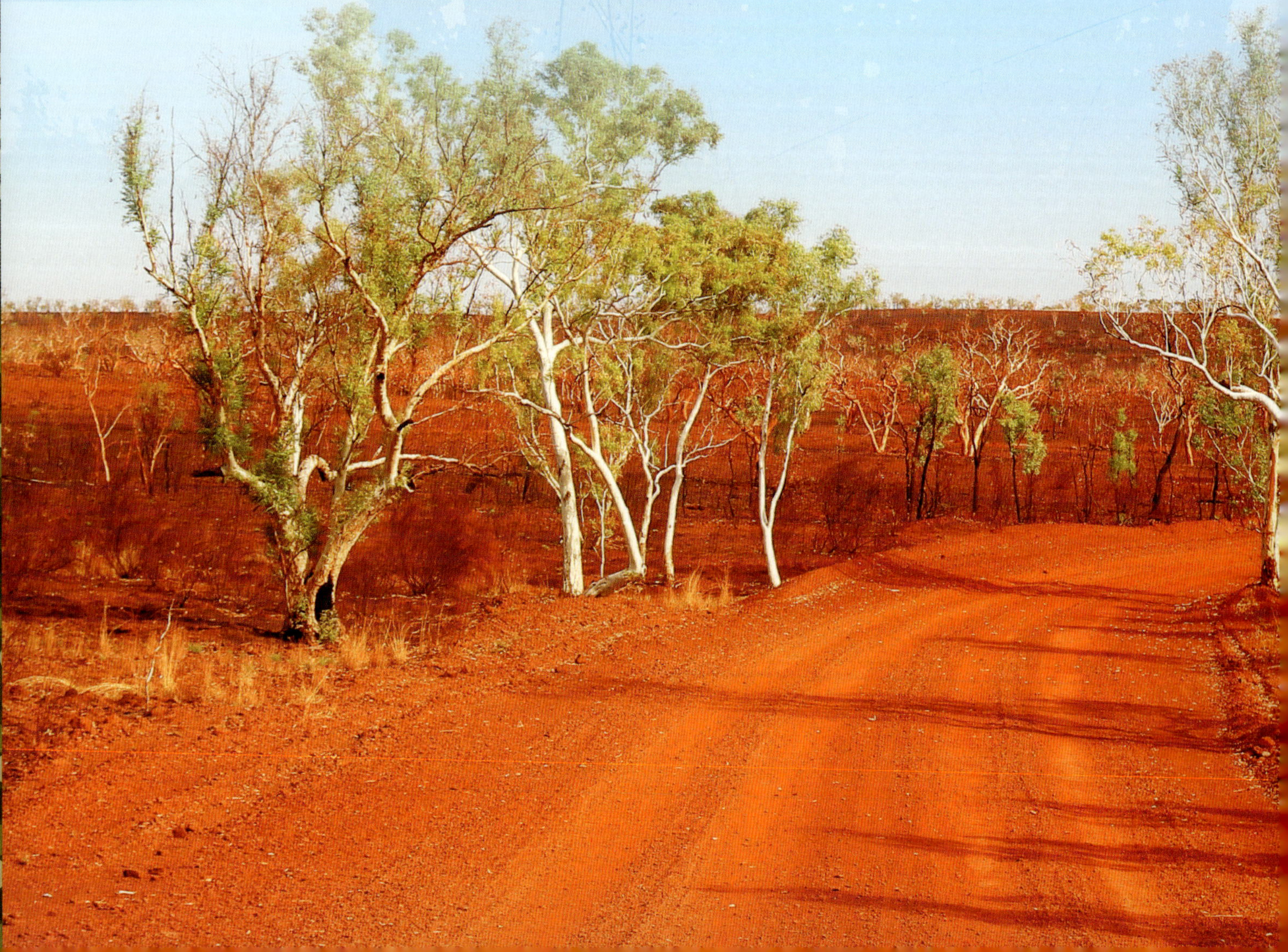

CONTENTS

Geography of Western Australia 4
Aboriginal History of Western Australia 6
Colonial History of Western Australia 8
Transport in Western Australia 10
The Mining State 12
Industry in Western Australia 14
Agriculture in Western Australia 16
Environment and Sustainability in Western Australia 18
Government of Western Australia 20
Notable People From Western Australia 22
Immigration to Western Australia 24
Major Sites in Western Australia 26
Flags, Symbols, Emblems and Special Days of Western Australia 28
How to Find Out More, Primary and Secondary Sources 30
Glossary and Index 32

Some words are shown in red, **like this**.
You can find out what they mean by
looking in the glossary.

Geography of Western Australia

Western Australia is the largest state of Australia. Perth on the Swan River is the capital city. The nearest countries are Indonesia and East Timor to the north.

There Are Nine Regions in Western Australia

1. Kimberley Region

In the far north of WA, the Kimberley has a monsoonal climate with high rainfall and high temperatures. With only about 40,000 people, this is one of the least populated areas on Earth. Off its coast are coral reefs, remote islands and an abundance of marine life, while inland are magnificent waterfalls and gorges. Broome in the Kimberley is well known for its beautiful Cable Beach and for its pearling industry.

2. Pilbara Region

The Pilbara is in the northwest of WA. Mining is important in this region of dry, red plains. Many of the mining workers do not live permanently in the Pilbara, but fly in for work.

3. Gascoyne Region

Wildflower tourism and salt mining are significant for the economy of the Gascoyne region which is in the northwest of WA. Visitors to Shark Bay and the Ningaloo Reef come to see the wildlife and explore the local national parks.

4. Goldfields-Esperance Region

The Goldfields-Esperance region is in the southwest of WA. The gold rush brought thousands of miners to Kalgoorlie and Murchison in the late 1800s. The area has a long agricultural history.

5. Great Southern Region

On the south coast of WA, the Great Southern region includes coastline, seaside towns, agricultural land and national parks.

6. Mid West Region

This region has the oldest rocks in the world, dating from four billion years ago. Its diverse economy includes mining, agriculture and tourism.

7. Peel Region

The Peel region is 75 kilometres south of Perth. It includes coastline as well as urban and agricultural land. The bauxite mine at Huntly is the world's largest.

8. South West Region

This is WA's most popular tourist destination. The Margaret River area is a centre for wineries and the spectacular limestone caves contain fossil remains of extinct animals.

9. Wheatbelt Region

In the south west of WA. Agriculture is the main industry in this region, but there is also mining, manufacturing, fishing and tourism. The Wheatbelt Way is a tourist route that reveals the history and natural beauty of the region.

FAST FACTS

Longest river
- Gascoyne River

Highest mountain
- Mt Meharry in the Hamersley Range

The northernmost place in WA
- Cape Londonderry

Population

There are about 2.6 million people in Western Australia and most of them live in Perth. The next biggest town is Bunbury with about 67,000 people. Small mining towns have changing populations depending on the health of the mining economy. Other larger towns in WA are Geraldton, Ellenbrook, Busselton and Kalgoorlie.

PREDICT THE POPULATION

Draw a graph using these figures. Can you use the graph to work out what the population of Western Australia might be in the year 2040?

YEAR	1860	1890	1920	1950	1980	2010	2040
POPULATION of WA	15,000	49,000	331,000	573,000	1,284,000	2,319,000	?

FAST FACTS

Highest recorded temperature in WA:
- **50.5° C at Mardie in 1998.**

Climate

Because Western Australia is so large it has a variety of climates.
NORTH - The climate is monsoonal with only two seasons, wet and dry.
NORTHWEST - Tropical cyclones have caused injuries, deaths and damage properties.
SOUTHEAST - The climate has wet winters and hot summers.

Deserts of Western Australia

These deserts are home to many plants and animals that have adapted to survive in the extreme, arid conditions.

- Great Victoria Desert
- Great Sandy Desert
- Tanami Desert
- Gibson Desert
- Little Sandy Desert

Islands of Western Australia

There are hundreds of islands off the coast. Here are a few of them:

- Rottnest Island
- Barrow Island
- Dirk Hartog Island
- Houtman Abrolhos Islands
- Monte Bello Islands
- Recherche Archipelago

DID YOU KNOW?

Between 1829 and 1837, the Indigenous population around Perth declined from about 1,500 to 295 people.

WORD FILE

bauxite - aluminium ore

Aboriginal History of Western Australia

Aboriginal people have lived in Australia for at least 60,000 years. They developed complex societies and ways of life, and their culture depends on having strong spiritual connections to the land.

There are many different Aboriginal nations, each with its own lands and cultural traditions. A nation is defined by its connection to its land and by its language. Groups within a nation may also have their own dialects.

New settlers in the Lower Warren District, 1912

European Settlers and the Aboriginal Nations

The Aboriginal nations had strong relationships with the land, and this caused conflict between them and the European settlers. Cattle and sheep replaced native food animals on the land, and settlers colonised areas for themselves that had been in traditional ownership for thousands of years.

Jandamarra

Jandamarra, a Banuba man, led a resistance movement against the settlers in the 1890s in the Kimberley area. He gained a reputation for having special powers, since he was able to escape capture so many times.

Yagan

Yagan, a Noongar man from the Perth area, is remembered today by the Noongar nation as a leader who fought for the traditional rights of his people over their land. He was killed in 1833. There is a Memorial Park to honour him in Belhus, Perth. The Noongar nation includes these groups:

- Yued
- Gnaala Karla Boodja
- South West Boojarah
- Wagyl Kaip
- Ballardong
- Whadjuk

PLACES

The Burrup Peninsula

The Burrup Peninsula, which is in the Murujuga National Park, has 10,000 examples of prehistoric rock art, and over 700 archaeological sites. The area is Yaburarra land.

Lake Argyle

A dam on the Ord River has now flooded the valley which was the land of the Mirriwung Gajjerong people. Lake Argyle was created to provide water for people and industry, and it has become one of the largest freshwater lakes in Australia.

Mulka's Cave

Mulka's Cave is near Wave Rock in Hyden, in the south west of the state. The name comes from an Aboriginal legend about a man named Mulka. The legend says he was a very large man and this is why the hand stencils in the cave are large and high up on the walls.

Burringurrah (Mount Augustus)

This enormous stone outcrop, the largest in the world, is twice the size of Uluru. It is on Wadjari land, in the Gascoyne Region, and is a well-known site for caves and Aboriginal rock art.

EVENTS

1946 Pilbara Stockmen's Strike

This strike lasted for three years and was the longest workers' strike in Australian history. The strike was coordinated by Aboriginal leaders Bin Bin Dooley and Clancy McKenna. They were seeking better pay and working conditions for Aboriginal stockmen.

Mowanjum Festival

This festival is a celebration and corroboree representing the Worrorra, Ngarinyin and Wunumbul people. It is held every year in July, near Derby. The meeting honours Wandjina, the supreme spirit being.

WORD FILE

colonise - to settle in a new land and impose a new culture on the people living there

traditional ownership - the Aboriginal land ownership system in existence before the arrival of Europeans

dialects- different forms of the one language

Colonial History of Western Australia

Timeline

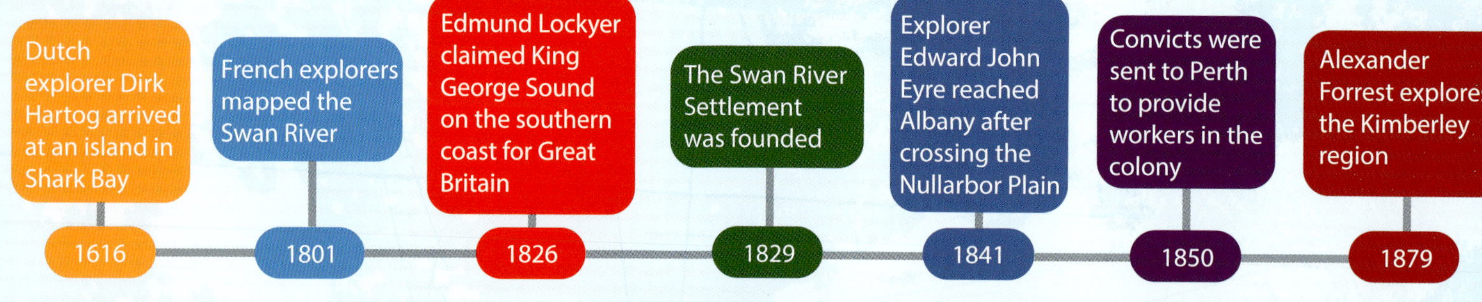

TIME TRAVELLER

Look at the painting of the foundation of Perth. Choose one person and imagine what they are thinking about the future.

Map of Swan River Settlement and Surrounding Country, 1831

Perth

To prepare the Swan River Settlement for colonists, the British government sent James Stirling, the first Governor, and John Septimus Roe, a surveyor, to choose sites for townships. They arrived in June 1829. In the following months other sailing ships arrived with settlers as passengers.

On 12th August 1829 the settlers held a small ceremony to declare the foundation of a town. Helen Dance, wife of the captain of the sailing ship, the Sulphur, marked a tree with an axe and it was then chopped down to show where the township was to be located.

Albany

Edmund Lockyer founded a small convict settlement at Albany in 1826, and claimed the western area of the Australian continent as a British colony.

Edmund Lockyer in uniform of Captain of the Sydney Volunteer Rifle Corps, Photograph taken before 1860

FAST FACTS

'Terra Australis' was the European name for Australia before it became a British colony

The First Governor of Western Australia

In 1829, Governor James Stirling arrived in the area that was to become Perth. In the beginning he governed a struggling settlement. It was the middle of winter and the new arrivals all had to live in tents, as there were not yet any buildings. The only food they had was what they had brought with them on ships. The Swan River Settlement struggled to grow crops and clear land for farming, but Stirling had succeeded in one of the main aims for them being there, which was to stop the French from claiming the land for France.

The Kimberley

In 1879, Alexander Forrest explored the Kimberley region and realised it was perfect for cattle grazing. His reports on the area resulted in the birth of the cattle industry in Western Australia's north. Based on his reports, cattle owners drove their livestock across from the eastern colonies and settled in the Kimberley region. Some of these journeys took years to complete and are legendary in the state's history.

Kalgoorlie and the Gold Rush

Patrick Hanna and two other Irish prospectors found a gold nugget at Mount Charlotte in Kalgoorlie in 1893. This was the start of Western Australia's gold rush. Thousands of people came to the area to search for their fortune. The wealth that came from gold mining resulted in a boom in business and building in the gold mining towns and spread to benefit many other areas of the state as well.

FAST FACTS

FIRST NEWSPAPER
The Perth Gazette's first issue was produced in 1833.

FIRST ELECTRIC TELEGRAPH
In 1869, Western Australia became the last colony of Australia to get a telegraph connection. People could finally contact each by sending telegrams rather than waiting for letters to arrive.

Settlers' Houses

The settlers lived in many different types of housing, depending on how wealthy they were and whether they had convicts or other labourers to help build their houses.

Bark and Slab Huts - A wooden frame covered in sheets of bark.
Wattle and Daub - A wooden frame plastered with a mixture of clay, straw and manure. Patrick Taylor Cottage in Albany was built with wattle and daub in 1832. It is the oldest surviving house in Western Australia and today is a museum.
Stone - One of the earliest advertisements in the Perth Gazette in 1833 was for the sale of a stone and weather-board house. This was only four years after Perth was founded.

Family outside bark hut

Transport in Western Australia

Pre-Colonial Transport

The first methods of transport used by Aboriginal people in Australia were walking and paddling canoes. Canoes were made of bark or from hollowed out logs, and they were used for fishing and to cross rivers and harbours. 'Canoe trees', which have large scars where bark was peeled from them, are reminders of this early technology. One of these trees is in Kings Park in Perth.

Roads

The early Swan River Settlement could only be reached by ship since there were no roads to it from any of the other Australian colonies. By 1950, the main road north of Geraldton, and the road to Kalgoorlie from Perth, were both only partly sealed. Many remote roads in the state are still unsealed.

Cobb & Co Coaches

As in other states, the Cobb & Co stage coaches provided public transport to remote parts of Western Australia. They were particularly in demand taking miners to the goldfields during the gold rush. While travel on these coaches was expensive and exhausting, they were once the only means of mass transport available.

TIME TRAVELLER

When the Eyre Highway across the Nullarbor Plain was just a dirt track, what were the dangers that people travelling on it faced?

The Eyre Highway

The Eyre Highway was constructed in 1942, but it remained a dirt road across the Nullarbor Plain in Western Australia until 1969. It is the main road connection with the eastern states.

Camels

Because camels could survive better than horses in Western Australia's arid areas, they were used from 1860 onwards for transport of goods to remote townships. Camels carried building materials for the Overland Telegraph and the Goldfields Water Supply project, and a number of explorers depended on camels to carry supplies. When road and rail transport improved, the camels were no longer needed and most were released into the bush. They have now become a pest in parts of the state.

River Transport

Perth was founded on the Swan River so that boats could use the waterway to transport people and goods to other settlements. The first jetty for Perth was built in 1842. Before this, boats had to be unloaded by carrying goods through the mud to the shore. Boat builders set up business along the river but this industry ceased in the 1930s when roads and motor vehicles replaced the river traffic.

Shipping Ports

The Port of Fremantle on the Swan River was founded in the same year as Perth. Today, 75% of all seaborne imports into Western Australia are unloaded at Fremantle. Mining exports are loaded at other ports along the west coast.

Port Hedland and Port Dampier are the first and second largest bulk ports in the world. They are located in the Pilbara region and the main export loaded is iron ore.

Air Transport

The lack of sealed roads, the annual floods during wet seasons in the north and the large distances involved have resulted in air transport becoming a necessity across Western Australia. The Australian government's Remote Air Services Subsidy Scheme makes travel and air freight more affordable for people in remote areas.

Trams

Electric trams started running in Perth in 1899. By 1952 they were removed, as motor vehicles and trains took over as people's preferred modes of transport around the city.

Railways

Railways made the transport of produce fast and simple, and they contributed to the economic development of the state. Western Australia has large networks of railroads that were built mainly to carry the products of mining and agriculture from the interior of the state to the ports on the coast. Two examples of these are the railway lines linking the Pilbara to Port Hedland, and the Wheatbelt railway lines for transporting grain to the ports. The first railway in the state was privately owned, carrying timber from Yokonip to Busselton. The carriages were pulled along the tracks by horses until a steam engine arrived. The first government owned railway line opened in 1879 and carried lead and copper ore, wool and passengers from Northampton to Geraldton on the coast. The residents of Perth did not get a railway line until 1881. The Trans Australian Railway, linking Western Australia with the other states, was built in 1917.

WORD FILE

bulk port - a port for the loading of large quantities of the one product, such as grain or iron ore

ore - rocks which can produce a mineral or metal

WA - The Mining State

Between 1938 and 1960, the Australian government banned all iron exports, saying that there might not be enough iron ore left to supply local needs. Since this restriction was lifted, the mining industry in Western Australia has boomed and contributed to economic prosperity throughout Australia.

Iron Ore

Exports of iron ore result in 70% of the state's total income from all types of mining, making Western Australia the second largest iron ore producer in the world. Most of the iron ore is purchased by China. 90% of Australia's iron ore reserves, at 54 billion tonnes, are in the Hamersley Range in the Pilbara region.

Petroleum (Crude Oil and Natural Gas)

Western Australia produces 71% of Australia's crude oil and 63% of the natural gas. Petroleum products come mainly from the Carnarvon, Perth and Canning Basins and from off-shore drilling on the North West Shelf. Shell's Liquefied Natural Gas (LNG) development in the northwest ocean will produce, store and transfer LNG, which is used for heating in homes and businesses and to fuel cars.

Gold

Western Australia is the source of over 70% of Australia's gold production, and has 18% of the world's gold reserves still in the ground. The Gold Rush of the 1890s has ended, but there is still enough gold in Western Australia to provide a major source of its mining income. The Goldfields-Esperance region is the main location where gold is mined in Western Australia.

Nickel

Nickel is Western Australia's fourth most valuable mineral. Nickel resists corrosion so it is useful for coating other metals and has been used to make coins. The only nickel mining in Australia is in Western Australia, which also has the world's largest reserves still in the ground.

Aluminium Ore (Bauxite)

Bauxite is Western Australia's third most valuable mineral. It is used to produce aluminium metal, which is the second most used metal in the world after steel. Bauxite is mined at Huntly, Boddington and Willowdale mines.

Base Metals

Copper, lead and zinc are produced from underground mining operations in Western Australia. Ore from the Golden Grove mine is shipped through the nearby Port of Geraldton to smelters in China, Japan, India, Thailand and Australia.

Mineral Sands

Mineral sands are a source of titanium metal and zirconium. They are mined in the southwest of the state and are exported mostly to China and the USA.

Asbestos

In 1943, the town of Wittenoom in the Pilbara was a thriving place based on the income from the asbestos mine. The whole area has now been declared contaminated as a result of the life-threatening effects of asbestos on anyone who comes into contact with it.

Diamonds

The Argyle Diamond Mine in the Kimberley produces beautiful pink diamonds for jewellery, as well as industrial diamonds. Production began in 1985 using open-cut mining which has now been replaced by underground mining. The electricity supply for the mining comes from the Ord Hydro Power Station.

Coal

Compared to other states, Western Australia's coal mining industry is not large. Most of the coal is mined at Collie where it is used to fuel the power stations generating electricity.

Uranium

Uranium is used as fuel for nuclear power stations, for weapons and in medical testing. Uranium has been found in the Northern Goldfields, the Pilbara and the Kimberley, but it has not yet been mined.

Mining Towns and Small Businesses

The value of the mining industry to Western Australia depends on world prices, since most of the ore and other products produced are exported. This means that the revenue received each year varies and the number of jobs can be affected. When fewer people are employed in an area, local businesses like shops and services can suffer.

THINK ABOUT IT

What makes uranium mining different?

- The Australian government imposes controls on who can buy uranium
- Any buyer must only use it for peaceful purposes
- The radioactive mining waste needs special disposal methods

WORD FILE

smelter - a factory which extracts metal from ore
revenue - money received

Industries and Business in Western Australia

Apart from mining, there are many other industries that contribute to the economy of Western Australia.

Tourism

Tourism is a large contributor to the economy of Western Australia, resulting in about $9 billion being spent by visitors from Australia and overseas. The variety of tourist destinations ranges from remote national parks to marine experiences and historic townships.

Lake Argyle

Created as part of the Ord River Irrigation Project, Lake Argyle is a local centre for water sports, swimming and recreational fishing. The nearby town of Kununurra is a base for tourists exploring the surrounding Kimberley area.

Wildflowers

Western Australia has many species of wildflowers that are not found anywhere else. Three of the places that tourists visit to enjoy them are Kings Park in Perth, the Fitzgerald River National Park and the Stirling Range National Park.

Cruise Shipping

Cruise shipping passengers make a substantial contribution to the state's economy each year. Cruises take advantage of Western Australia's scenic coastline and also depart for other states and countries.

The Pearling Industry

The town of Cossack on the north coast became a centre for the pearl shell industry in the 1860s. By the 1900s Broome had taken over this role. The divers were Aboriginal, Japanese, Malaysian, Chinese and other people from the Indian Ocean region. At first they collected the pearl shells without using any diving equipment, but later they used heavy diving suits supplied with air pumps.

The pearl shell was used for buttons and household items, After plastic was invented, Broome began to concentrate on the production of pearls for jewellery. The cultured pearl industry in Western Australia now produces 80% of the world's cultured South Sea Pearls.

FAST FACT

The pearl oyster has a tiny crab that lives inside the shell. The crab keeps the oyster clean and healthy.

Energy

The remoteness of so many of its communities and mining operations means that Western Australia has a large number of privately owned electricity generators, using diesel and solar power. Coal, gas and diesel supply the fuel for most of the government's electricity generators. The Ord Hydro Power Station was built in 1966. It supplies Wyndham, Kununurra and the Argyle Diamond Mine.

Shipbuilding

The Australian Marine Complex in Perth repairs, maintains and builds ships and offshore oil and gas equipment. It is the largest marine industrial complex in Australia and its floating dock allows large vessels to be lifted and repaired. The shipbuilding facilities are able to construct yachts, fast ferries, rescue, patrol, fishing or military vessels.

Small Businesses

97% of all businesses in Western Australia are in the small business category. Most of them are in building and construction, while the next largest groups provide professional and scientific services, real estate services and financial services.

Salt

Salt is produced from sea water in Dampier, Port Hedland, Lake MacLeod and Shark Bay. Large evaporation ponds rely on the sun to dry off the water and leave behind the salt crystals. Most of the salt is exported and used in industry.

Agriculture in Western Australia

Western Australia aims to develop a reputation as a clean and green state, with agriculture that is free from pests and diseases.

The Ord River Irrigation Project

In 1972, the Ord River Dam created Lake Argyle and provided water for agriculture in the Kimberley region. The nearby town of Kununurra was built as the service centre for the irrigation project, which includes both the Ord River Dam and the Kununurra Dam.

FAST FACTS

- Lake Argyle holds over 18 times more water than Sydney Harbour
- There are 35,000 freshwater crocodiles in the lake

The Wheatbelt Region

Wheat is grown mainly in the Wheatbelt region and is Western Australia's largest agricultural income earner. Indonesia is one of the state's export markets for wheat, while Japan also uses it for udon noodle production.

Other Crops

Although wheat is the largest crop, farmers also grow barley, carrots, canola, lupins and oats. Most of this produce is used locally except for barley and carrots. Barley is used in China, Japan and India to produce beer, and in the Middle East to feed animals. Carrots are exported to South East Asia and the Middle East.

Cattle and Sheep

Beef Cattle

Both live cattle and meat are exported to South East Asia. The cattle raised in the Kimberley are mostly for live export. Those raised on the southern pastures are destined for packaged meat export markets.

Sheep

80% of all the sheep and lamb meat produced in Western Australia is exported overseas. The biggest markets are China and Saudi Arabia. Some of the sheep raised are exported live to countries in the Middle East.

Dairy Cattle

The dairy industry is located in the far south west of the state. The milk produced is mostly used locally.

Bees & Honey

Honeybees in Western Australia are free from the pests, mites and diseases found in eastern Australia and other parts of the world. The health of its bees is a result of strong biosecurity measures and makes Western Australia a favoured source for honey and queen bees.

Fishing

Western Australia produces rock lobsters, prawns, abalone and scallops. Inland, at Lake Argyle, commercial fishing supplies the Perth market with catfish. Some of these are up to 1.5 metres long and weigh 40 kilograms.

Wool

The fine Merino wool produced by sheep farmers is used mainly for clothing. 83% of the wool exported goes to China and 9% to India.

Horticulture

Horticultural crops are grown in parts of the state that are well irrigated or have high rainfalls. These places include the Ord River Irrigation Area in the north, the Gascoyne region, the outer parts of Perth and the south west region. Crops include fruits, vegetables, wines grapes and flowers. Western Australia produces two thirds of Australia's exported strawberries.

Wine

Wine grapes are grown in the southwest of the state, in the Margaret River area. Produced by small businesses, the fine wines from Western Australia are renowned for their quality.

WORD FILE

horticulture - growing plants in gardens, orchards and nurseries

Environment and Sustainability in Western Australia

Sustainable practices for agriculture and industry require a balance between using the land and waterways for development and keeping areas as regions of natural beauty. The protection of endangered plants and animals is also important.

Bush Fires

The Department of Fire and Emergency Services regulates controlled burning and provides community education on bush fires. The worst bushfires in the state occurred in 1960 - 1961 in the southwest area when a number of towns were destroyed.

RESOURCES	HOW WE CAN LOOK AFTER THEM
SOIL	Correct use of fertilisers and avoiding soil erosion
WATER	Keep water supplies unpolluted
NATIVE PLANTS	Avoid complete clearing of areas for pastures
NATIVE ANIMALS	Keep some areas of natural bushland for food and shelter
AIR QUALITY	Avoid polluting the air through poor industrial practices

Protecting Native Plants and Animals

Endangered animals in Western Australia are affected by habitat loss, introduced species, infectious diseases, fire and climate change. Some of these animals are the bilby, numbat and quokka.

Sustainable Fishing

The state government controls commercial and recreational fishing to ensure fish stocks and their habitats are not destroyed.

The Ord River

When the dam was built on the Ord River, the natural environment for the local wildlife changed. Some animals drowned in the flooding of the area, while others increased in numbers due to having a constant supply of fresh water.

National Parks

Western Australia has 100 national parks, 13 marine parks and extensive conservation reserves.

Pearling

Pearling is regulated by the government to ensure the sustainability of the industry. As well as relying on wild oysters, the industry also operates hatcheries which produce baby oysters for transfer into the open ocean to grow.

Renewable Energy

Renewable sources of energy can come from water, wind and solar power.

- **The Ord Hydro Power Station** - Uses water power to produce electricity for the local area and the Argyle Diamond Mine.
- **Wind Farms** - There are three large wind farms in the state that together generate 65% of Western Australia's renewable energy.

Water

Drinking water comes from dams, rivers, rainwater tanks, desalination and bores. The Perth Seawater Desalination Plant was completed in 2006. It supplies 17% of Perth's water needs and uses electricity from wind farms to ensure it runs sustainably.

Mining

While mining can be very destructive to the environment, some mining operations, like the ones at Barrow Island, take care to ensure that the wildlife and environment are minimally affected. Barrow Island, off the Pilbara coast, is a large oil and gas field. Since 1910 it has also been a nature reserve.

FAST FACTS

There are more wild camels in Australia than anywhere else in the world. They ruin water-holes and fences and compete with native animals for food.

PESKY PESTS

- Feral camels and donkeys
- Rainbow Lorikeets
- Cane Toads
- Ferrets
- Crows

Biosecurity

Western Australia is free of many pests and diseases that are found elsewhere in Australia and throughout the world. There are strict rules for bringing animals, fruit, vegetables, nuts, seeds, plants and bees into the state. Any imported machinery or tools have to be cleaned of all soil and plant material. Quarantine inspectors at interstate borders check for any items that might pose a biosecurity threat. The State Barrier Fence stops pest animals crossing into Western Australia. This 1,170 kilometre fence extends from Kalbarri in the north to Jerdacuttup in the south.

WORD FILE

sustainability - ability of the environment to be used without being destroyed
quarantine - isolating dangerous plants, animals and diseases
biosecurity - controlling plants, insects and animals that are harmful

Government of Western Australia

Timeline Before Federation

Before 1829 The Aboriginal nations throughout Western Australia governed according to their own laws

1829 James Stirling was the first governor of the Swan River Settlement

1832 The first Legislative Council had four members appointed by the Governor

Ships at the Swan River

1867 Free adult males who owned property could vote for the Legislative Council

1890 Bicameral parliament formed, having a Legislative Assembly and Legislative Council

1899 Women were allowed to vote

1901 Federation resulted in Western Australia changing from a colony into a state

FAST FACTS

'Terra Nullius'

These Latin words mean 'land that nobody owns'. The British government used this idea to allow them to claim land in Western Australia.

Timeline After Federation

1920 Women could stand for election

1921 Edith Cowan became the first woman elected to the parliament

1962 Aboriginal Australians could vote

1964 Before this date only land owners could vote for the Legislative Council

1973 People over the age of 18 could vote

Premiers of Western Australia

Sir John Forrest became the first Premier of Western Australia in 1890. The first woman to become a state Premier in Australia was Dr Carmen Lawrence in 1990.

Parliament House

This building was begun in 1902. The stained glass windows were made in Perth and local jarrah timber is used throughout.

Sir John Forrest, first premier of Western Australia, 1897

Local Government

There are 140 local governments in Western Australia, including those for the Cocos (Keeling) Islands and for Christmas Island. Postal voting for local government elections is used widely because many people live in remote areas.

The Western Australian Parliament Today

The Legislative Council (Upper House) has 36 members
The Legislative Assembly (Lower House) has 59 members.
They meet in Parliament House in Perth.

WORD FILE

bicameral - a government having two houses or sections

Notable People from Western Australia

Aboriginal Leaders

Ken Colbung (1931 - 2010) Born on the Moore River Native Settlement. He served as a sergeant in the army and later became an activist for indigenous rights, resulting in him being recognised with an MBE and Order of Australia for his services to the Aboriginal community. As one of the Nyungar leaders, he worked for the return of the head of the warrior Yagan from the British Museum.

Albert Barunga (1910? - 1977) A leader of the Worora people, Barunga assisted Charles Kingsford Smith who was forced to land his aircraft, the Southern Cross, near the Glenelg River in 1929. He also guided navy ships on coastal patrols during World War II, and helped to translate the Bible into the Worora language.

Science

Barry Marshall (1951 -) Born in Kalgoorlie, Professor Marshall received the Nobel Prize in 2005 for discovering that stomach ulcers can be caused by helicobacter bacteria.

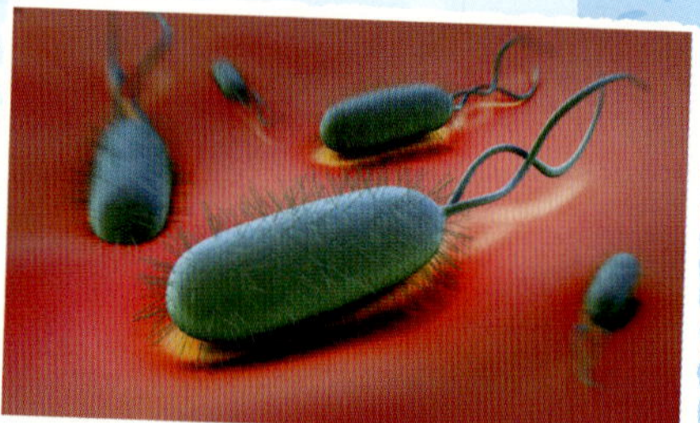

Helicobacter bacteria.

MAKE YOUR OWN LIST

Who are three people you think are important in your family, school or suburb?

Politics

Edith Cowan (1861 - 1932) Born in Geraldton, Cowan was the first woman member of the Western Australian parliament. She introduced reforms for women, children and in education. A university is named after her, and her image is on the $50 note.

John Forrest (1847 - 1918) Born in Bunbury, Forrest became the first Premier of Western Australia in 1890. He was also an explorer and led the first overland expedition from Perth to Adelaide in 1870.

Sport

Herb Elliott (1938 -) Born in Perth, Elliott is a runner who held the record for the 1,500 metre and the mile races. He won gold at the 1958 Commonwealth Games and 1960 Olympics.

Walter Lindrum
(1898 - 1960) Born in Kalgoorlie. An expert billiards player who became the world champion. When he retired in 1950, he had won 57 world titles.

Louise Sauvage (1973 -) Born in 1973 in Perth, Louise Sauvage has won gold medals for Australia in wheelchair racing at the Paralympic Games, the World Athletics Championships and a number of marathons around the world. She works to inspire young disabled athletes, and her motto is, 'You'll never know what you can do or achieve until you try.'

Writing

Shaun Tan (1974 -) Born in Perth, Tan is a best-selling children's book author and a film maker. He won an Academy Award in 2011 for his animated film The Lost Thing.

Tim Winton (1960 -) Born in Karrinyup, Tim Winton is a writer of novels for children and adults. His work has won many awards, including the Australian Vogel Award and the Miles Franklin Award. The settings for his novels are often inspired by his home state of Western Australia, where he has become a campaigner on environmental issues.

Sally Morgan (1951 -) Born in Perth, Morgan has received awards for her children's books and art. After overcoming initial criticism of her painting style, she discovered her Aboriginal heritage and this inspired her success.

Immigration to Western Australia

People have come from around the world to live and work in Western Australia, and have contributed to the social diversity of the state.

60,000 Years Ago

The ancestors of the Australian Aboriginal people arrived from the north and spread throughout the country. The northern parts of Australia were connected to other landmasses 8,000 years ago, when the sea levels were lower than they are today, and people could travel easily across the shallow seas.

Britain

The first free British settlers arrived at the Swan River in 1829. They wanted to develop the new colony without convicts, but had to accept 10,000 of them from 1850 to 1868 to provide the workers needed for building and agriculture. The convicts' guards were given land grants and became some of the earliest settlers.

A lack of workers was always a problem in the development of Western Australia. As a result, in 1923, the government encouraged 75,000 British migrants to take up wheat farming in the Wheatbelt.

Emigration in search of a husband, 1833

China

Chinese came to Western Australia during the gold rush, and also worked in the pearling industry. In the early 1900s, their market gardens supplied most of the vegetables grown in the state.

Japan

Japanese pearl divers were vital to the pearling industry in Broome, where there is an historic Japanese cemetery. Japanese later developed the cultured pearl industry in the area.

Afghanistan

In Wyndham there is an old cemetery in which all the graves face towards Mecca. The graves are those of the Afghan camel owners who once provided a freight service across the isolated parts of Western Australia.

Main Roads Migrant Camp in Narrogin

This camp was home to many migrants who arrived from Europe after the Second World War and up until the 1950s. The camp had tents and Nissen Huts, which were made out of corrugated iron. The migrants worked on building roads and railways for the state and local governments.

Welcome Walls

The Western Australian Museum has constructed two Welcome Walls listing the names of migrants who came to the state by sea. The Welcome Walls are at Fremantle and Albany.

Western Australia Today

Most of the people in the state who were born overseas have come from Great Britain. In recent years, many people have also arrived from New Zealand, China, India, Italy, South Africa and Malaysia.

OTHER COUNTRIES

Migrants to Western Australia have come from many other countries apart from the ones listed above. How many can you name?

Major Sites in Western Australia

These sites include buildings, structures and natural features. They are important for their beauty, rarity and their historic connections.

Shark Bay

Shark Bay became Western Australia's first world heritage listed area in 1991. Visitors flock to hand feed dolphins at Monkey Mia, and to see the stromatolites at Hamelin Pool. The seagrass beds in the bay feed 10% of the world's dugongs, while Shell Beach is covered in tiny shells for over 120 kilometres.

Bungle Bungle Range

The unusual landscape of the Bungle Bungles includes thousands of large mounds coloured with red, orange and black bands. These rocks are 350 million years old.

Ningaloo Reef

This coral reef attracts dolphins, dugongs and whales. Divers can swim with huge Whale Sharks, some measuring up to 18 metres long.

Fremantle Prison

Building of this colonial prison began in 1852 to house the convicts who were transported to Western Australia from 1850. Fremantle was chosen as the prison site rather than Perth because the convict labourers were needed to help build the shipping port there. The buildings retain many of their original features, allowing us to see the way that colonial prisoners had to live.

FAST FACTS

There are four World Heritage Sites in Western Australia:

1. **Shark Bay**
2. **Bungle Bungle Range – Purnululu National Park**
3. **Ningaloo Reef**
4. **Fremantle Prison**

The Nullarbor Plain

The Nullarbor Plain begins near Kalgoorlie and extends into South Australia. The name comes from Latin words meaning 'treeless'. The Nullarbor has very harsh weather conditions and for many years contributed to Western Australia's isolation from the eastern states. The Eyre Highway now makes crossing the Nullarbor a safer journey than it used to be.

The Indian Pacific Train Service from Perth to Sydney across the Nullarbor is one of the world's great train journeys. Travellers may see some of the 100,000 wild camels which are descended from those used to carry construction materials when the railway was first built.

Cossack

The town of Cossack in the northwest was a centre for the pearling industry in the 1860s and was later a port for the surrounding areas. It is now a ghost town and a fascinating tourist destination with old buildings maintained as museums.

The Bibbulmun Track

This 1,000 kilometre track is a bush walking trail. It was opened in 1998 and runs from Kalamunda to Albany. The Bibbulmun Track has received a number of tourism awards.

The Porongurup Range

The Porongurup Range is in the southwest region. At over a million years old, it one of the oldest mountain ranges in the world. The Granite Skywalk, perched on Castle Rock, provides a sweeping view of the area.

Flags, Symbols, Emblems and Special Days of Western Australia

People living in Western Australia use flags, symbols and special days to show their connection to their community. These connections include pride for the group they belong to, an interest in the history of their group or area, and wanting to join others for celebrations that bring people together.

Western Australian State Flag

The Union Jack in the corner is a reminder of the historical connection with Great Britain. The swan is the state's bird emblem and is also a reminder of the founding of the colony on the Swan River.

RULES FOR FLYING THESE FLAGS

- **Don't fly more than one on the same pole**
- **Don't fly them in the dark**
- **Raise the flag to the top of the pole before lowering it to half-mast**
- **Treat these flags with respect**

Australian Aboriginal Flag

The Aboriginal Flag was first flown in 1971. It was designed by Elder Harold Thomas.
Yellow disc - the sun and yellow ochre
Red - the land
Black - the Aboriginal people of Australia

Special Days

Australia Day - On 26th January each year, Australians commemorate the founding of a British colony by Governor Phillip at Sydney Cove in 1788.
ANZAC Day - Ceremonies and marches for ANZAC Day are held all around the state on 25th April each year. The largest march in the state is in Perth.
NAIDOC Week - A week in July each year to celebrate the history, culture and achievements of Aboriginal and Torres Strait Islander peoples. Communities and government bodies organise events around the state for NAIDOC Week.
Western Australia Day - Formerly known as Foundation Day, this public holiday is held on the first Monday in June each year to commemorate the founding of the Swan River Colony in 1829.

Symbols of Western Australia

Floral Emblem - Mangles' kangaroo paw
Animal Emblem - Numbat
Bird Emblem - Black swan
Marine Emblem - Whale shark
Fossil Emblem - Gogo fish

The Coat of Arms

This is a symbol of Western Australia and each part of it has a meaning.
Kangaroos - represent the wildlife
Boomerangs - represent the Aboriginal people
Black Swan on Blue Water - represents the founding of the colony on the Swan River
Crown - represents the connection with Great Britain
Flowers - Mangles' kangaroo paws are the floral emblem of WA

Make Your Own Coat of Arms

Design a Coat of Arms for your family, suburb or sport group, etc.

- Use symbols that everyone will know
- Your own Coat of Arms could include drawings or pictures to tell the history of the group
- Think about where to use your Coat of Arms
- Where have you seen the Western Australia Coat of Arms used?

WORD FILE

Elder - a respected Aboriginal person who is a custodian of traditional knowledge
half-mast - flying a flag halfway up the pole as a mark of respect when a community leader dies

How to Find Out More
Primary and Secondary Sources

There are many ways to find out more about Western Australia. You can do this using both primary and secondary sources. Websites can have a mixture of both types of sources on them.

Primary Sources

- **Interviews** - when people say what they have seen
- **Letters** - when the writer was the person experiencing the event
- **Newspapers** - when the facts are presented
- **Photos** - when they have not been altered
- **Maps**
- **Old Items & Antiques**
- **News on Television** - when it shows pictures of real events or a person saying what they have seen
- **School Newsletters** - when they list names or dates of events
- **Videos on Youtube or Facebook** - when they show an event and have not been altered

Secondary Sources

- **Letters** - when the writer is retelling the facts that someone else told them
- **Newspapers** - when the story is told by someone who retells the facts that someone else told them
- **Photos** - when the photo has been altered
- **Songs, Poems, Stories**
- **News on Television** - when it is reported by a journalist who did not experience the events

Fun Activities Using Sources

- Find old newspapers at your local library. Use these to look at pictures of areas you know and see how they have changed over time.
- Take photos of your school, paste them into an exercise book, add some notes and ask the librarian to add your book to the collection. This will then become a primary source for students in the future.
- Ask students and teachers to tell you what they know about the history of your school. Type the results into a Word document, print it and staple the pages into a booklet. You now have a secondary source for people to use in the future. Ask the librarian to add your booklet to the library collection.
- See if your town or school has been mentioned in parliament by searching its name in the Hansard record. Go to www.parliament.wa.gov.au and click on the 'Hansard' tab.

Museums

Visit museums to look at primary sources. For instance, you could look for examples of clothing that rich and poor people wore, or different modes of transport throughout history.

Museums in Western Australia

- The Western Australian Museum, Perth
- The Western Australian Maritime Museum, Fremantle
- Fremantle Prison Museum
- Bassendean Rail Transport Museum
- Durack Homestead Museum, the Kimberley
- The DFES Education and Heritage Centre in the historic Perth Central Fire Station

Western Australia Maritime Museum

Your Own Family and Friends

Primary sources do not always have to be about famous people. Interviews with your family and friends are important too. Your grandmother might recall what your suburb used to be like. Friends can share stories about coming to live in Western Australia either from other states or from a country overseas.

Websites

- Western Australian Department of the Premier and Cabinet www.dpc.wa.gov.au
- Australia's North West www.australiasnorthwest.com
- Western Australian Parliament www.parliament.wa.gov.au
- Lake Argyle www.lakeargyle.com
- Western Australian Department of Mines and Petroleum www.dmp.wa.gov.au

WORD FILE

Hansard - a record of what the politicians say in parliament

Glossary

bauxite - aluminium ore
bicameral - a government having two houses or sections
biosecurity - controlling plants, insects and animals that are harmful
bulk port - a port for the loading of large quantities of the one product, such as grain or iron ore
colonise - to settle in a new land and impose a new culture on the people living there
dialects - different forms of the one language
diversity - a range of differences
Elder - a respected Aboriginal person who is a custodian of traditional knowledge
half-mast - flying a flag halfway up the pole as a mark of respect when a community leader dies
Hansard - a record of what the politicians say in parliament
horticulture - growing plants in gardens, orchards and nurseries
ore - rocks which can produce a mineral or metal
quarantine - isolating dangerous plants, animals and diseases
revenue - money received
smelter - a factory which extracts metal from ore
sustainability - ability of the environment to be used without being destroyed
traditional ownership - the Aboriginal land ownership system in existence before the arrival of Europeans

Index

camels 10,19,24,27
Cobb & Co 10
deserts 5
gold rush 4,9,10,12,24
Jandamarra 6
Ord River 7,13-19
Stirling, James 8,9,20
Terra Australis 8
Terra Nullius 20
Yagan 6,22

www.redbackpublishing.com.au